THE CHRISTIAN'S SONG

MIKAYLA PINDER

WESTBOW
PRESS®
A DIVISION OF THOMAS NELSON
& ZONDERVAN

WestBow Press books may be ordered through booksellers or by contacting:

WestBow Press
A Division of Thomas Nelson & Zondervan
1663 Liberty Drive
Bloomington, IN 47403
www.westbowpress.com
844-714-3454

Interior Image Credit: Mikayla Pinder

All Scripture quotations are taken from the King James Version.

ISBN: 978-1-6642-4374-3 (sc)
ISBN: 978-1-6642-4376-7 (hc)
ISBN: 978-1-6642-4375-0 (e)

Library of Congress Control Number: 2021917724

Print information available on the last page.

WestBow Press rev. date: 09/27/2021

Dedication

"To my parents, for always loving me, supporting me, and instructing me in the ways of the Lord. I love you with all my heart!"

Contents

The Christian's Song

There's a peace and there's a joy
That no silver coin can buy.
There's a love not bound by limit,
And a faith that'll never die.
There's a hope beyond all measure
And a glory, yes, on high.
Yes, that's the Christian song.

There's a life, oh, everlasting
And a freedom from all sin.
There's a God who paid the ransom
For the fallen ways of men.
In our place, he died and suffered,
But in three days rose again.
Yes, that's the Christian song.

There's a realm unknown to sorrow,
Hidden from death and fear and cold.
There's a place of handsome mansions
And broad streets of solid gold.
There's reward but for his chosen,
And a world and wealth untold.
Yes, that's the Christian song.

There's a message and a mission
To ourselves we cannot keep.
We must share his gospel yonder
With the lost and wandering sheep.
Again, our Lord is coming,
So rise up and sow and reap.
Yes, that's the Christian song.

For God So Loved the World[1]

A star glows with full ardor
At the wonder of your birth.
O glory in the highest,
And peace to men on earth.
The heavens are rejoicing,
And the angels fill the skies.
The Father's face is dancing
As he gazes in your eyes.

His heart lies in that manger,
His very best, his all.
The wholeness of salvation
In a precious babe so small,
A sacrifice of love
Wrapped in redemption's plan.
Will evil bruise your heel
And pierce these tiny hands?

Will your own reject the promise
Of the seed of Abraham?
Will they crucify the body
Of the holy great I Am?
Yes, you'll crush the serpent's head,
And you'll overcome the grave.
And these fallen souls of sinners
From the judgment will be saved.

But the pathway to your triumph
Is the cruelty of the cross.
And the Father's heart is racing

---

[1] John 3:16.

As it undertakes the cost.
May this sphere of clay be broken
As he pours out all his soul,
And your purpose be accomplished
As declared within the scroll.

And then it will be finished,
And one day we will believe.
And freedom and salvation,
One day we will receive.
And then we will not perish
In the darkness of the night,
But live, oh, everlasting
In the glory of your light.

Sing, Bethlehem

Your Christ has come,
Born in a trough of straw.
The heavens ring,
Behold your King.
Be filled with breathless awe.

Sing, Bethlehem.
The star above
Has crowned your longing earth,
And God's good grace
Has filled your space
With the joy of his Son's birth.

Sing, Bethlehem.
The virgin's child
Has come to break your chains.
Your void hearts fill,
And blind eyes heal
And cleanse your crimson stains.

Sing, Bethlehem.
Your Lord above
Descended to your ground.
The Prince of light
Is born tonight,
So lift a gladsome sound.

The Good Shepherd's Heart

My thoughts about you are countless.
They outnumber the stars above.
I call each star by name.
They are all kindled with my love.

Like infinite crystal faces
Of a celestial prism, they shine.
With silent voices as one proclaim
My goodness and glory divine.

Lost lamb, I'm calling you by name
With an ardor that knows no bound.
I numbered each fine strand of silk
Sprouted from your mortal crown.

And if not one sparrow can fall
Outside my affection's space,
How much more do I care for you?
How more abundant is my grace?

I left the ninety-nine to find you
My throne beyond the crystal sea,
The streets of gold for streets of dust,
My seat of splendid royalty.

To descend to your afflicted ground
And bear your sorrows in my frame.
The rule that Adam lost to night,
With you in mind I set to claim.

They pierced my hands and pierced my side,
But my face I set like flint.
My jealous pursuit of your soul.
My love would not relent.

I paid the final price for you.
My all with all I gave.
Then I rose in joyous victory
And overcame death and the grave.

I'm knocking at your soul's own door.
My love is still zealous in this fight.
The joy of the award still flames
The spirit of its light.

Dear straying one, return to me.
My staff will keep you from all harm
I long to lift you 'round my neck
And welcome you with waiting arms.

Behold the Lamb of God

Oh, see the gift of heaven.
He walks upon this sod.
Here comes the Prince of angels.
Here comes the Son of God.

Son of Judah, son of David,
Son of expectation.
King of all who was and is.
Lord of all creation.

Hosanna in the highest
To the One who'll set us free.
Holy Lamb of Israel,
Why chose to come to me?

A Testimony of Grace

Hear the rushing of the crowd.
Hear the anguish in her cry.
See the torrents of despair
Rush from her guilty eyes.
The disgrace of her trespass
Her soul cannot deny.
The law calls out for justice;
Now a sinner, she must die.

Her accusers' rage is thirsty
To make her pay the price.
But they bring her before Jesus
To test his sound advice.
Their hands reach out for stones
As their words strive to entice
The God who seeks their mercy
And not their sacrifice.

The Teacher's voice is silent
As he writes upon the sand.
A mystery of heaven
He spells out with his hand.
But an answer to their question
His enemies demand.
So with the power of the Spirit,
To his feet he finally stands.

His tongue declares the wisdom
Of the One upon the throne.
He speaks, "Let he who has no sin

Now cast the first stone."[2]
Their consciences condemn them.
Their plots are overthrown.
One by one they slip away,
The accused now left alone.

"Woman, where are your accusers?"[3]
She looks around the place.
"Does nobody condemn you?"[4]
Behold the empty space!
"No, Lord," she quickly answers,[5]
A smile blooms on her face.
How he who has no sin
Still shows such wondrous grace!

"Neither do I condemn you.
Now go and sin no more."[6]
Now the woman walks away,
Not as she was before.
A soul set free from judgment,
A broken heart restored.
A witness of the goodness
And the mercy of our Lord.

---

[2] John 8:7.
[3] John 8:10.
[4] John 8:10.
[5] John 8:11.
[6] John 8:11.

Mary's Alabaster Box

In unified haste
Their heads turned her way.
In concord they raised
Their rage for display.
All moved as if by
A conductor's bidding.
Her type, their hostile
Remarks forbidding.

Eagerly their judgments
Gleamed in their eyes
As a woman like she
Approached the Christ.
Uninvited, she dared
And entered the room.
A sight as arresting
As her costly perfume.

The Lord was there with them.
They didn't know,
But the sinner knew,
And her faith drove her so.
The spears of their tongues
Could never contend.
Their blindness she could
Care less to offend.

The time raced with haste
As her pounding heart beat.
She stepped on the waves
And refused to retreat.
This moment divine

May never repeat.
She anointed his head
And knelt at his feet.

She wept, and they saw.
And she didn't care.
She dried his feet
With the veil of her hair.
How could their minds grasp
In what darkness she dwelt?
How could they relate
To the love that she felt?

'Twas not their own soul
That once was so lost?
How could they e'er fathom
Her gratitude's cost?
Her heart never reached
The door of her lips,
But her tears caught the heed
Of the Lord in its grip.

His compassion compelled,
He answered her faith
And shamed those
Who berated her with such hate.
Her broken request
He gladly embraced.
The whole of her debt
He forever erased.

Her chains were undone.
Her soul was set free.
The weight of her past

Now swept in the sea
In the tide of mercy,
In the ocean of grace.
How peace filled her heart,
And joy filled her face!

Her story lives still,
Our hearts to inspire
The drive in our steps
And fuel in our fire.
May we step on the waves
And never retreat.
Our moments appointed
May never repeat.

Such Love!

Is it true, Prince of heaven,
Son of God, was it for me
You took a crown of biting thorns
And gave your crown of glory?

Did you take the Roman scourge
That tore with iron fangs,
A brood of charging vipers
That screamed with hateful clangs?

Did you take the cross, the nails,
And labor o'er each burning breath?
And for a sinful wretch as I
Hang your guiltless head in death?

Such love! Such purest selfless love!
Such mystery, such power divine!
It sets my heart from prison free
But shakes the structure of my mind!

My Mind but Grasp a Narrow Part

What sinful eye behold thy face?
What mortal mind perceive thy grace?
What futile reason know thy heart?
My mind but grasp a narrow part!

What human tongue thy love describe?
What perfect praise my hand ascribe?
Thy fullness speak, how can I dare?
Thy glory far beyond compare.

Thy majesty all bounds exhaust,
Why look on I, a speck of dust?
What worth thou find, this earthen heart?
What care thou set my soul apart?

What love compelled thee leave thy throne?
What grace to dwell among my own!
Why my soul thou came to save?
Why for me thy life thou gave?

Why the suffering? Why the cross?
Why my sin thou paid the cost?
Why thou plead my desperate case?
Why the mercy? Why the grace?

Why the passion? Why the zeal?
Why my life thou sought to heal?
Oh, the goodness of thy heart
My mind but grasp a narrow part!

It Is Finished

There he gave his final breath
On the brow of Calvary.
The paradox of God and man,
Like a lamb was slain for me.
Fallen for my trespass,
He descended to Sheol,
The cherished Prince of heaven
On the frontline for my soul.

A canopy of darkness
Overwhelmed the sunlight's path.
Groans of anguished heaven
Struck like flashing swords of wrath
It is finished!
Lo the wonder
As the sacred curtain tore.
The chasm twixt the throne and man
Now done forevermore.

Three days of mournful heaving,
Three nights of heavy tears.
Three moments that would climax
All our earthly doubts and fears.
In the crossfires of the unseen,
In the trenches of the grave,
A warrior was battling
With a love that wouldn't wave.

The Spirit roared within him,
Like the shouting host of Zion,
How death who bruised the spotless Lamb
Now shook before the lion!

How the serpent's head was crushed
By the heel of the stronger!
The keys of stolen paradise,
The darkness held no longer.

Now ascends the mighty Savior
In most splendid victory
As the stone upon the entrance
Of the tomb makes haste to flee.
Here walks in new authority
The feet of him who bled.
The holy Christ, the blessed Lord,
Is risen from the dead!

The angels burst with jubilee,
Their brilliant banners raise.
With one voice of awe and rapture,
All creation lifts his praise.
And heaven kisses earth
As the hues of daybreak blush,
And a trance of surreal wonder
Follows grace's boundless rush.

The hearts of those once bound
Sing with keen intensity
In joyous adoration
Of the One who set them free.
Hope crowns their newfound faith
As their past is done away,
And evil lies defeated
Beneath love's eternal ray.

The victor is alive!
All power his now and forever.
How he embraces the reward
Of his most honorable endeavor!
It is finished!
It is finished!
The battle has been won!
Eternal exaltation
To the resurrected Son!

Resurrection Morning

Quick as the rays of daybreak bloom,
There stirs within the cave.
The King, enclosed in Joseph's tomb,
Now rises from the grave.
He steps with triumph 'pon his land,
Redeemed with selfless love,
And waves the key high in his hand
All pow'r low and above.

Swift is the wind to sweep his praise
O'er rushing plain and mount.
How rapid all is set ablaze!
How glorious the fount!
The blood that cries eternally
Forgiveness for our wrong.
Great shame torments the enemy.
How gladsome Zion's song!

Inflamed with wondrous victory,
The angel rolls the stone.
How nature shouts with jubilee!
All doubts and tears disown.
Hallelujah! He is risen!
Rushing waves of grace pulsate,
Freeing those enchained in prison
From Sheol's defeated gate.

How great God's love upon our earth!
How powerful his arm!
What boundless joy attends new birth!
What beauty and what charm!

He lives in us and us in him;
Our ways are bound to thrive.
His Spirit floods our vessel's brim.
King Jesus is alive!

All Glory Belongs to Jesus

All glory belongs to Jesus,
All praise and adoration.
How beautiful the worship
That ascends from His creation!

The chorus of a thousand tongues
All unified as one,
Lifting up the King of kings,
The resurrected Son.

All power belongs to Jesus.
All hail His matchless name.
His arrows are like lightning.
His eyes are burning flames.

The armies of a thousand kings
Are crushed beneath His might.
The champion of victory
Has never lost a fight.

All wisdoms belongs to Jesus,
All mystery divine.
His throne endures forever.[7]
His justice always shines.

Let everything with breath
With all their heart and soul,
The worthy Lamb of heaven,
Forevermore extol!

---

[7] Psalm 45:6.

Our Roads to Emmaus

The Lord is always with us,
Though we don't oft recognize
The Shepherd of our beings,
Like a traveler in disguise.

When he speaks, the breath of heaven
Sweeps our souls to boundless heights,
And the shades of gray obscurity
Turn to blooming hues of light.

The pieces come together
As the image becomes clearer,
And our doubts are wiped away
Like a fog from a mirror.

And his lamp leads us onward
As our road climbs, falls, and turns,
And our faith encounters fire
As our hearts begin to burn.

But oftentimes we're too consumed
With the griefs that weigh us down.
We do not seem to notice
His identity profound.

But as he journeys with us onward
And breaks the bread divine,
The rays of revelation
Shine upon our wakened minds.

Soon we realize that the one
Who turned our darkness into day
Is the resurrected Son of God,
Who was with us all the way.

The hand of God was working.
How could our eyes have missed?
How glad we are to know at last
The Lord was in our midst!

Pilgrim's Praise

On the summits of the mountains
I will praise him with my voice.
In the shadow of the valleys
I still have reason to rejoice.

I was once a wretched sinner,
But Jesus came and now I'm found.
He redeemed me from my trespass
And set my feet on solid ground.

And if he does naught else for me
As I trek toward gates divine,
This pilgrim is equipped with all
The fire for the finish line.

My name is in the Book of Life.
What despair can I afford?
I am on the way eternal.
Oh, hallelujah! Praise the Lord!

Holy Spirit, Blessed Friend

Your will helps me adhere.
Please guide me to the end.
And whisper in my ear
The way that I should go.
As I step out on the wave
In my thirsty valleys, blow
And call me from the grave.

Baptize me with thy fire;
In this willing temple, dwell.
As I tarry, come draw nigher.
Give me water from your well.
Help me soar on eagle's wings.
Let your presence now descend.
Your mercies, my life sings,
Holy Spirit, blessed friend.

Precious Savior, Come This Hour

Stretch thine hands scarred with love.
May thy sacred fount of power
Flood my heart from its source above.

May thy crying stripes on Calv'ry
Cry out still my wounds to heal.
Blessed right to heirs of roy'lty,
To my longing now reveal.

On my sores of this realm fallen
Lay thine hands that healed the blind.
Hearken now my fervid calling.
Your sure words my soul remind.

Touches of thy wondrous pity
Touch me like the sleeping maid.
Raise me from these ashes dreary.
May my hope rest in your shade.

In my vale make yourself bigger.
Cause my eyes to see the sun.
Resurrect my fading vigor.
Make my crippled legs to run.

Make me dance on waves of glory.
Make me soar on eagle's wings.
May thine wonders be my story
As your grace in my life rings.

Rings the bells of newest mercies,
Stirs the pool of thy grace above.
Precious Savior, come this hour.
Stretch thine hands of sacred love.

When I Read the Bible

A match of holy fire
Lights the wick of my heart.
The shadows flee with terror,
And the Red Sea blows apart.

Blinding fogs evaporate,
Like dew on sunlit days.
A lamp of divine guidance
Illuminates my ways.

Each burning word speaks volumes
To my hungry soul within.
Still waters reflect heaven
As you confirm time again.

The sword uproots the schemes of man
And rends the drapes of night.
And streams of joy inundate my face
As I glory in your light.

May My Eyes Be Ever Fixed on You

On you and you alone.
On wayside steep or valley deep,
Or high upon life's throne.

May my eyes never leave your lead
And look on some vain thing.
May no distraction come before
My love for you, my King.

May no harsh light or blackened night
Blind my faithful gaze.
May all my focus be on you
Throughout my journey's days.

I'll follow you with all my heart,
With all my soul and might.
My eyes will hold firmly to you.
Pray never leave my sight.

Lily of the Valley

Tell me, lily of the valley,
Who spun your snowy gown?
Purer than the silver gems
On the midnight hour's crown.

Even the silks of Solomon
Weren't as lovely as your own.[8]
Even the scents from Sheba's land
Could not rival your cologne.

Tell me, lily of the valley,
Do you sweat for your attire?
Which today is for the woodland's pride
And tomorrow for the fire.[9]

How great your maker cares for you!
How great he cares for me!
How great his blessings he bestows
And love without degree!

---

8 Matthew 6:29
9 Matthew 6:30

This Is the Day

This is the day the Lord has made,
    So let us now rejoice.
His mercies over all still reign,
    So with cause we lift our voice.
In thanksgiving to our Father,
    Who supplies our daily bread,
Who leads us by still waters,
    And pours oil on our heads,
Whose angel goes before us,
    Robed in power most divine.
He turns our mourning into dancing
    And our water into wine.
May your will be our desire;
    May you guide our every choice.
This is the day the Lord has made,
    So let us now rejoice.

For Day and for Night

Lord, I thank you for each beautiful day,
When the sun was in bloom and light was my way.
Green was the pasture, joy was my song,
Still were the waters; no more did I long.

Lord, I thank you for each hard and dark night,
When to praise was to burn and to breathe was a fight.
When trust was a cross, and my prayers were all tears.
When deep was the valley, then I knew you were near.

Lord, I thank you for all, the sun and the rain,
The smiles and laughter, and heartache and pain.
Each morning you're faithful, your mercies are new.
Each night I learn to depend more on you.

7:45

I wake up as the day before.
The fog immerses me once more.
My hopes are scattered on the floor.
I'm groping, hoping towards the door.

I'm scared to stop and scared to fall,
Scared I'll hit another wall.
Dear Lord, regard my urgent call,
And be right with me through it all.

Please guide me through this unsure space,
And hold me in your warm embrace.
Please help me persist in my race,
And light my way with wondrous grace.

Lord, Save Me

One day I'm on the mountaintop;
One day I'm in the vale.
Both a heaven and a heaviness
Beyond all words to tell.

One moment I'm on top the sea,
The next I am beneath.
Lord, save me from these hungry waves
And death's ever-tearing teeth.

My thoughts and doubts are screaming why.
My power fails to think.
My faith is swarmed with billows high.
It's beginning now to sink.

The ocean dares to swallow me;
I'm caught between its jaws.
Scarcely do I catch my breath
When it strikes me with its claws.

It pulls me toward its roaring core,
And the darkness closes in.
Lord, hear my cries of deep distress,
And save me once again.

Savior, please stretch out your hand;
I know you're in control.
Don't let the rage of the proud waves
Now overwhelm my soul.

Don't let me fall prey to its teeth.
My help is in you, Lord.
Like a bird, I will escape the snare,[10]
And my faith will be restored.

Help me walk on top these waves;
Uphold me with your grace.
You're bigger, yes, than all my fears
And every storm I face.

[10] Psalm 124:7

On Top of Every Storm

We set sail in the night
On a sea with a mask,
As calm as a dove
As still as glass.
But at the turn of the watch,
She tore off her veil,
Exposing a face
That threatened to kill.

With unjustified anger,
She stirred up her soul,
Scheming and daring
To swallow us whole.
She battered our boat
And shattered our masts,
And shredded our sails
With violent blasts.

At the height of that storm
In the black of the night,
Came approaching a figure,
A ghostly sight.
Like one star in the sky
Or moonlight on the sea,
He came walking on the waves
Of dark Galilee.

There was a glow 'bout his face
And a peace in his stride,
Unmoved by the tempest
In the face of the tide.
The lightning raged sore

About the gray skies
But could not outshine
The light in his eyes.

The might of the storm
Could no more compete.
The great ocean bowed
'Neath the greater one's feet.
He spoke with such power,
"It is I; be of good cheer."[11]
My faith stirred to life;
He silenced my fear.

He called me to come,
And I jumped, and I came.
And I walked in the power
Of his wonderful name.
And as long as my eyes
Are fixed fast on his form,
I'll conquer and I'll walk
On top of every storm.

---

[11] Matthew 14:27.

Your Still, Small Voice

O fleeting feet, grow still again.
O anxious heart, grow calm within.
A gentle whisper grips my soul.
It's louder than the stirring wind.
O breath of heaven, now descend,
This weary wanderer console.

Why am I here? I ran in fear.
I cried and longed for death so dear.
But your still voice brought peace divine.
At once, my doubts were disengaged.
The mountain shook, the fire raged,
But only one could seize my mind.

Oh, meet me in the mountain's cleft,
And fill my dying lungs with breath.
Come share with me your words of grace.
Just speak, my dark will turn to light.
Your word can stir these bones to life.
Come find me in the secret place.

Yahweh, Fight for Me

I'm waiting in your temple, Lord,
Attend my earnest plea.
Relieve my soul,
Behold the scroll.
O Yahweh, fight for me.

How this horde seeks to devour,
Like the rushing of the sea!
Their words blaspheme;
Their weapons gleam.
O Yahweh, fight for me.

Destroy their forts of arrogance.
Condemn their tongues, Most High.
Your glory show
Like the dark billow
On the crown of Mount Sinai.

Deliver us now once again.
Divide the stretching sea.
Their boasts disgrace,
Their plots erase.
O Yahweh, fight for me.

Now release your mighty angel
And still the lion's roar.
Your name defend.
You'll do again
What you have done before.

And all will know that you are God.
Yours is the victory.
Move, burning lamp,
Disturb their camp.
O Yahweh, fight for me.

Exodus

Our moving is his moving.
O shout with joyful cry.
The terrors of the Nile,
Forever bid goodbye.

We're marching out in freedom.
The Lord is on our side.
The fury of his mighty fists
Has shattered Pharaoh's pride.

He plagued our land of bondage
And broke its iron back.
We go with full provision;
There's nothing that we lack.

His cloud is there before us,
Like a shield around our host.
His hand is our protection,
Like the blood upon the post.

The Lord is fighting for us.
Each breath is like a roar.
Our enemies we see today,
We'll see them now no more.

Yes, nothing is impossible.
He'll lead us through the sea
And to our land of promise
In triumphant victory.

The Promised Land

My heart in surety beyond the Jordan dwells
Where my eyes have yet to taste the pleasure.
A fruitful land where untold goodness swells,
And milk and honey without measure.
Green are the meadows there, still are the waters.
Oh, that my feet would dance where faith has possessed!
Oh, that I could sing with the sons and daughters
Ceaseless hymns of praise to the One most blessed!
How much longer must I wander this ground
And bear the sting of those who failed to trust?
Eagerly I await the trumpet's sound
When these earthen walls will crumble to dust.
Then I'll inherit my promised reward,
And live evermore in the land of the Lord.

By His Spirit

Lord, lead us once again.
With the pillar and the smoke,
Let the mountain melt like wax,[12]
And the oil break the yoke.
Let the Jordan flee before us,
Like the waters of the sea.
O Captain of the holy host,
Please grant us victory.

There stands the mighty city,
Like a fortress in the mount.
And the banks are overflowing
With the rushing of the fount.
The gates are tightly shut,
But the Lord is on our side.
And the tablets in the ark
Are our manna and our guide.

The hearts of those against us
Are as silent as the dead.
And the title deed is granted
To wherever we shall tread.
Obediently we'll march,
And with awe we'll lift our praise
To the Ruler of the heavens
And the Ancient of all days.

Yes, nothing is impossible.
We lean not on our might.
By his Spirit we will conquer,

---

[12] Psalm 97:5.

By his Spirit we will fight.
The sacred text will happen
Just as its author planned.
He'll lead us to our destiny,
Into our promised land.

Is Anything Too Hard for Me?

Is anything too hard for me?
The King of all eternity,
I laid the cornerstone of earth.
I clothed it in fine robes azure,
The heavens sang, the angels stirred
At the rapture of its birth.

I painted billows in the sky
And lit the flame in morning's eye.
I lull the lamp of day to sleep.
I formed the bond in Pleiades' stars,
And locked the sea in iron bars
To guard the treasures of the deep.

I wrote the laws of dawn and noon
And built the abode of the moon.
My word inflamed its silver rays.
The glory of the night I crowned.
I satisfy the thirsting ground.
All of creation sings my praise.

My hand can hold the galaxy.
One breath can part the deepest sea.
My voice is like an army's roar;
The mountains quake with fear below.
I breach the fort of hail and snow.
The weapons I reserve for war.[13]

---
[13] Job 38:22–23.

I fight against those who fight mine.
The ribs of life my touch entwined.
I raise the dead soul from the grave.
Where there's no escape, I am the door.
On wings of untold heights I soar.
I dance atop the wind and wave.

The sores of man my stripes still heal.
The nations bow before my will.
I set the bound from prison free.
I took the keys of fallen death
And fill the dry bones with my breath.
There's naught at all too hard for me!

David and Goliath

A lion once attacked my sheep.
Another roars against Saul's keep.
The past and present are transparent.
The call of the Lord is inerrant.
He gives me strength.
The first I slew.
This raging beast I'll conquer too.
A higher motive stirs within.
My God has moved; he'll move again.

He's bigger than this fiend I face.
I will not fear or be disgraced.
I'd sooner dread the fate of ten,
Whose faith was in the flaws of men,
Than live my life in dark regret
And fall back to stifling Egypt.
My trust is in the sovereign Lord.
These cowards' doubts I can't afford.

The greater lion in me roars.
It's he who trains my hands for war.
To the insect's height I cannot stoop,
With God, I can run through a troop.[14]
With him, I can scale any wall.[15]
He makes me dance on mountains tall.
He yet remains unstoppable,
The King of the impossible.

---

[14] Psalm 18:29.
[15] Psalm 18:29.

This giant fights with sword and spear,
But I in he whose name I fear,
I'm armed with more than stone and sling.
The battle is the Lord's I sing.
He'll grant me triumph on this sod,
So all will know there is a God.
Goliath's height may striking be,
Hence weigh the fruits of victory.

Nehemiah's Courage

'Neath the golden rays of heaven
Or the curtain of the night,
Our eager hands aren't ceasing
To rebuild the ruined site.
Each breaking of the morning star
Unveils its swelling height.

The flame of heat can't stop us.
The billows' tears may fall.
Our enemies sound war cries,
But we're not moved at all.
We have one hand on our weapons
And one hand to our wall.

Yes, the Lord of heaven's armies
Gave us favor from the King,
And the praises of his power
In Mount Zion ever ring.
We abide beneath his shadow[16]
And take refuge 'neath his wing.[17]

So we carry on with courage.
Lo our faith is standing tall.
We know how to gain victory
And triumph over all.
With one hand on our sword, his Word,
And one hand to our wall.

---

[16] Psalm 91:1.
[17] Psalm 91:4.

When God Is on Your Side

Twenty pieces of silver gleaming
With the lightning of a sword
To silence two dreams of one.
How they raised their spears of envy
Against the one they abhorred,
Against Jacob's favored son!

They rent his robe of rich brilliance.
Their scoffs echoed his lament.
They sold their own as a slave.
How foolish their nearsighted minds!
Did they think they could prevent
The dreams the Sovereign gave?

Their plots were cruel and evil,
But God was working out his plan
And ordering his servant's steps.
How grace can overcome all wrong!
How divine the mighty hand
To arrange what would come next!

From Potiphar's house to the prison
To the palace of esteem,
His blessed purpose at last!
The lives of many souls were saved
When God gives you a dream.
Be sure it'll come to pass!

Four centuries of sore agony,
The scourge of Pharaoh reigned.
Israel groaned beneath its yoke.
Their cries pierced the celestial heart.

Four hundred years of grievous pain.
Then the Lord Almighty spoke

Ten plagues subdued the Nile's land.
Ten warnings to the pharaoh
To set his beloved free.
How his hand unveiled its wonders!
How his power overflowed
As he split the mighty sea!

With a cloud, he led his host onward.
How glad the sons and daughters!
There was nothing that they lacked;
Their oppression now behind them.
When God divides the waters,
There is no turning back!

Their pursuers fell defeated.
Their foes they saw that day.
They saw them now no more.
How they danced to the Promised Land!
No mountain can stand in your way
When God opens a door!

When your enemies attack you,
They'll stumble, flee, and hide.
Their schemes will be confused.
How their weapons will fail to prosper![18]
Nothing can stand against you
When God is on your side!

---

[18] Isaiah 54:17.

Father, Forgive Them

"Father, forgive," the Savior cried.
He spoke with love even as he died.
He prayed for those who scorned his face.
They pierced his hands;
He showed them grace.

A crown of thorns was upon his head.
"They know not what they do," he said.[19]
They ripped his back with scourge and lead.
It pleased them that he grieved and bled.

Their eyes were blind;
Their souls were lost.
They nailed their King upon the cross.
They spat upon his sacred bod.
They crucified the Lamb of God

Forgive!
He cried out for the throng.
Forgive!
He cried for all men's wrongs.
Forgive!
He cleared my guilty name.
Forgive!
Lord, help me do the same.

---

[19] Luke 23:34.

Peter's Resolve

His Spirit came upon me,
Like a mighty rushing wind.
The fire of the promise
On my bowed head did descend.

And rivers of the Spirit
Overflowed these lips of clay.
He commanded me to preach his Word;
I cannot but obey.

The masses are enlivened
With the freedom of the flame.
They turn to Christ, the Savior,
And are baptized in his name.

The sick are cured completely,
And the poor have been supplied.
Some seek to be enfolded
By my shadow passing by.

Now they wish me to be silenced.
But I know I'm not alone.
This is the hand of heaven
And not of my mortal own.

Their words are bitter arrows
As they whisper in the ear.
The One who rules from judgment's seat
Is not the one they fear.

The wrath of blinding envy
Has their fallen hearts well stirred.
But I cannot help but to declare
All that I've seen and heard.

Their threats are but fleeting dust
That I shake, not carefully.
I know a fourth man in the flame
Who is standing next to me.

They sell their frail integrity
As they seek to crush my frame.
They bow before the statue
Of cheap pride and worldly fame.

But like those who faced the furnace,
My faith they can't uproot.
I'll stand though they raise a sound
With the scourge or with the flute.

What can mere flesh to do me?
My help is in the Lord.
To whom else shall I go to?
His life is my reward.

They heat the furnace hotter
As they grope in foolish sin.
The fervor of the fire
Can't compare to this within.

The God I serve is able
To save me from their plans.[20]
He'll send his mighty angel
And snatch me from their hands.

But even if he doesn't,
My stubborn faith won't sway.
His Spirit has commanded;
I cannot but obey.

---

[20] Daniel 3:17.

Noah's Day

How aimless were their straying thoughts!
Shooting stars of galloping pace,
Rushing gusts with no finish line
On the horizon of their race.

Their acts were like untamed fire.
Their hands were enslaved to their minds.
Prisoners bound with willingness
To whate'er their lusts inclined.

They feasted their short time away
And drank their shame into the grave.
They groped on the dark path they chose
And scoffed at Noah's ark to save.

Then the waters burst upon them,
And the flood unbarred its waiting doors.
The heaven roared with holy anger
And unleashed its mighty pours.

Suddenly they sank;
Quickly they cried.
But lo their fate;
They were too late!
What a lesson we can gather.
Let us not make our souls wait.

Let us choose the narrow way of light,
And build no more on sinking sand.
Let us turn from sin and turn to God
For his kingdom is at hand.

He Is Coming Back Again

Our Lord is coming back again,
And when we do not know.
But we're waiting and we're praying
For the sounding trump to blow.

An aura of expectancy
Glows like halos in our eyes.
The signs of the fulfillment
Wave like banners in the skies.

Our lamps are ever burning
With the oil and the light.
He'll return when least expected,
Like the striking thief at night.[21]

He's trampling out the wine press,
So be cleansed from all your stains.
Come to the feet of Jesus,
And be freed from evil's chains.

On bended knee receive Him.
Let His Spirit dwell within.
Keep watch with full awareness.
He is coming back again.

---

[21] Second Peter 3:10.

Love Is the Greatest

Eyes of eagles, tongues of angels,
Keys of envied mystery.
To what being are they gainful,
To what service shall they be
If love's fingerprint is absent?
Left behind the stage's veil
Aims of virtue sorely misspent.
Rays of light by clouds concealed.

Love is kind, and love is patient,
Selfless in its every hope.
Faith and action made adjacent
In the spotlight of time's scope.
In the face of dark affliction,
Love is faithful to endure.
Giving itself without restriction,
In the fire, sterling pure.

Present wealth and wisdom dearer
Shall depart with this domain,
Useless with perfection's mirror.
But the greatest will remain,
Everlasting, ever certain.
Nature of the One above,
Love in essence is a person.
As the Word says, "God is love."[22]

---

[22] First John 4:8.

Broken Sacrifice

Like autumn leaves we fade and fall.
Your sanctity our rags appall.
We trod in tainted skin.
Its stirs me in my dreams at night
And haunts me in the dawning light.
O wretched is our sin.

Have mercy on this soul, oh God,
Create a clean heart in this bod.
Please purify my wrong.
Wash me in redemption's flow,
And make my stains as white as snow.
Restore my joyous song.

O dweller of the heavens,
Don't cast me from Your presence.
My frame is frail and weak.
With flesh, we war, in dust exist.
Our breaths are like the morning mist.
My brokenness is all You seek.

Behold the pieces of my heart,
Upon the altar, rent apart.
Accept my sacrifice.
Repentance is my humble cry.
A broken soul, You can't deny.
None other will suffice.

The Sinner's Prayer

In the hands of the blessed Savior
I place all that I own.
I confess that I'm a sinner
As I kneel before your throne.

I ask for your forgiveness
And repent of all my wrongs.
I welcome you into my life.
To you I now belong.

I believe you died upon the cross.
For my guilt, your blood was shed.
I believed they laid you in the tomb.
Then you rose up from the dead.

I vow to serve you all my days.
May your Spirit dwell within.
May you use this willing vessel.
In your name I pray. Amen!

Here I Am

May the altar of surrender
Be the abode where I dwell.
May this willing heart be tender
And bid these worldly cares farewell.

Adieu to treasures overprized.
These dusty aims conformed to death.
Lord, let me see as through your eyes.
Fill my spirit with your breath.

Here I am and all that I own.
Nail my will upon the cross.
All selfish wants I fain disown
For your heartbeat for the lost.

Humbly I embrace the call
With full flame your servant sends.
I know you will reward my hands
And be with me to the end.

Victory in Gethsemane

His heart is full and heavy.
His soul is vexed to death.
There is blood on his brow,
And sighs with every breath.

For cursed humanity,
On cursed human sod,
In a shell of human dust
Here walks the Son of God.

Here kneels the Prince of heaven.
Here prays the Holy One.
"Father, take this cup from me,
But let your will be done."[23]

That cup is awful bitter.
His is the power to resign.
He holds the keys of all to come,
Yet, "Your will be done, not mine."[24]

Three times, "Your will be done."
Hark! Hang the cross, the grave
That resurrection morning.
Our souls from judgment saved.

Hang all Christ's work on Calvary,
And final victory
Upon that meek surrender
In dark Gethsemane.

---

[23] Luke 22:42.
[24] Luke 22:42.

Pray we be like Jesus
And triumph o'er Calvary
With our yes to his will
In our own Gethsemane.

I Surrender

I lay everything I am
Upon the altar again.
The biddings of this world can't drown
This calling deep within.
What futile time I've wasted
Building forts with feeble sand!
They've all crumbled 'neath the blow
Of the tide's sweeping hand.

I'm faint with all this fighting,
So now claim me as your own.
Mold this stubborn piece of clay,
And melt my heart of stone.
Your will will always triumph,
So I raise my white flag high.
The fading treasures of this sphere,
I wave them all goodbye.

Your love pierced through my heart
That I felt was bulletproof.
And you widened my horizon
As you split my prison roof.
The reward of my surrender
Will by far outweigh the cost.
So with joy I chase your shadow
As I bear my passing cross.

Living Water

My heart was both heavy and empty.
My soul was a lost ship at sea,
Tossed with waves of discontentment,
Seeking to quench that thirst in me.

I drank, and then I longed for more.
Yet the more I drank, the more I died.
My world was swallowed up with darkness,
And oft I feared and oft I cried.

Floods of shame oppressed my lungs
As I drowned in deepest sin.
Then I drank the Savior's living water
And did never thirst again.

His light burst upon my darkness
And turned my mourning into joy.
The wonder of his saving power
My tongue will ever now employ.

I'm alive;
I'm more than alive!
The old has now been cast aside.
My purpose is sure, my hope revived.
His well springs within;
I'm satisfied.

Give Me Jesus!

Give me Jesus, give me Jesus!
I want no worldly pleasure.
His love is light, his name is life,
His Word, a living treasure.

Give me Jesus, give me Jesus!
This world's an empty place.
I want the presence of my Savior.
I want his smiling face.

I want to see his heart,
Inhale his wondrous majesty.
I want to hear his gentle voice
And feel him breathe his life in me.

Give me Jesus! Give me Jesus!
This world has no reward
As sweet and pure and ever sure
As the glory of my Lord!

How Can My Tongue Refrain?

I got a peace I can't explain.
I'm filled with joy I can't contain.
Christ's blood redeemed my every stain.
How can my tongue, my song, refrain?

His mercies over all still reign.
He holds me through the peace and pain,
And breaks the grasp of every chain.
How can my tongue, my song, refrain?

He pours his blessings down like rain.
And fills my cup, yes, time again.
I'm filled with thanks I can't contain.
How can my tongue, my song, refrain?

How I Love You, Jesus!

Your presence is all I want.
It's where I belong.
I'm enraptured by Your love.
Taken prisoner
By Your unabating tenacity
To hold me and never let me go.

Your grace never fails to amaze me.
I find myself helplessly falling
Towards the gravity of Your heart.
Gasping for breath
In the ocean of Your affection.
B r o k e n
Beneath the weight of Your mercy.

I'm overwhelmed
By the compassion in Your eyes.
It's like trying to behold the sun.
Your every breath is life.
Your very essence is goodness.
Everything about you is beautiful.

Your thoughts about me are countless.
How I love you in return!
How I live to sing your goodness!
How I cherish your presence!
How I praise you with everything in me!
How I love you, Jesus!

The Heavens Declare the Glory of God[25]

Now I awaken to the kiss
Of the gold of the sky.
An ornament suspended
On the word of the Most High.
And this ground is swept in its arms,
Like a ship on the sea.
Were my eyes once so blind
That its light I could not see?

Nothing below can take shelter
From the warmth of its rays.
The craftsmanship of its artist
Its presence displays.
New mercies it speaks of he
Whom I once paid no thought.
But at last, my soul is awake
For my life has been bought.

How plain is his signature
On the banner above!
With azure ink he spelled
The infinity of his love.
A canvas of blue where dwells
The hushed heavenly voices.
A canopy where the silver stars
Dance and moon rejoices.

How was I not sooner provoked
Behind my prison bars
By such heights of freedom?

---

[25] Psalm 19:1.

Why did I cling to chains, to scars?
Now I embrace the praises
Of this celestial art
That drive me ever closer
To my Creator's heart.

And the sea! Was it always
So full of vigor and life?
And yet in this fallen sphere,
How much more beauty than strife!
I see reflections of heaven
In its vast crystal glass.
I hear the depth of God's glory
Proclaimed in its blast.

And as long as his faithfulness
Follows me all my days,
I'll join the choir of nature
And shout his worthy praise.
I've been saved and made alive!
Now I see as through new lenses
How beautiful our world!
How great the flow that cleanses!

And on the mount or in the valley,
My praises will ascend.
His goodness I will sing
With the bird and with the wind.
With the flowers, I will dance.
With the trees, I'll stand in awe.
Each new day brings a new reason
To employ my dropping jaw.

The veil has been torn, so I soar
Like the worm on stained glass.
And gone like last night's shadow
Is the stain of my past.
My life has been ransomed.
I'm taken by all that I see.
How beautiful is everything
Now that I am made free!

For Such a Time as This[26]

O orphaned daughter of Israel,
O maid of low degree,
Behold your time.
The heaven's chimes
Sound forth your destiny.

You'll siege the fort of the king's heart
And save your own from death.
Your face so fair
And cascade hair
Will vaporize his breath.

Your cheeks bloom like the buds of spring.
Your smile like pearls enthrall.
Your voice so sweet
And words discreet
Will plane his crumbling wall.

The arrows of your charming glance
Will strike his core as dead.
His fate embrace.
He can't but place
The crown upon your head.

O queen, hearken your cousin's cry.
How Haman beats his fists!
Your people mourn,
But you were born
For such a time as this.

---

[26] Esther 4:14.

The guidance of a hand divine
Has sent you to this throne.
So dry your tears
And do not fear,
For you are not alone.

Expose the serpent's cunning,
And brave the law of death.
Your banquet sort
Enter the court
With a prayer under your breath.

Put on your robes of royalty
And deck your saffron wrists.
Your face adorn.
Fair, you were born
For such a time as this!

Send for David

Send for the youth neglected
Out in the open field.
The mighty king of Israel
In a lowly field concealed.

Come, sun-kissed son of Jesse,
Come strike your charming lyre.
The One who reigns from heaven's throne
Has filled you with his fire.

He saw how you've been faithful
As you watched your father's sheep.
Now the wandering flock of Jacob
He is calling you to keep.

A warrior he was making,
Though your own were not aware.
He delivered both into your hands,
The lion and the bear.

He led you by the waters,
And he kept you through the vale.
He'll spread a feast and choose the least.
I dare to say he will.

The prophet now has filled his horn,
So rise up from this soil.
Go and God will fill your cup
And anoint your head with oil.

Encourage Yourself

The smoke may rise like clouds of fading faith,
And streams of grief may swallow up your strength.
Close friends may whisper words as sharp as swords.
But dare to encourage yourself in the Lord.

O son of Jesse, he who crowned your head
Will not forsake you now for dead.
Your heart may beat with the roar of a drum,
But lift your eyes to where your help comes from.[27]

Dare to hope even when there is no cause.
He who saved you from the lion's claws
Will help you overtake this raiding band
And deliver them into your hand.

With the Spirit, you will doubtless win.
God has done it before; he'll do it again.
You'll recover all, so gird your sword.
David, encourage yourself in the Lord.

---

[27] Psalm 121:1.

Can These Dry Bones Live?[28]

Can these dry bones live?
These frames of open death,
Can he who breathed in Adam's lungs
Fill them with his breath?

Can hope now stir to life
In the craters of the valley?
Can the scattered sons of Judah
To their land of promise rally?

The Father's wrath is brewing
For the justice of your cries.
There is lightning in his arrows
And a furnace in his eyes.

His fury struck the waters,
And the river turned to blood.
And he led his people onward
Through the pathway of the flood.

The foolish host pursued them.
But he looked down from the cloud
And threw their racing wheels
Into the tumult of the crowd.

Your children crossed on over.
Then Moses stretched his hand,
And the billows closed upon them
And washed them on the sand.

---

[28] Ezekiel 37:3.

And wonder filled the spirits
Of the brand plucked from the Nile.
And you'll rescue us again
From our stifling graves of exile.

Now remnant breathe, now receive.
Now prophet prophesy.
Now hope revive, now Spirit rise
And fill us with your life.

Lazarus, Come Forth![29]

Surrendered son of buried hope,
Hear the Son of heaven calling.
Feel the warmth of the daylight's rays
Fill the space where you have fallen.

The stone has been taken away,
Like a mount thrown in the sea,
Like the waters that were divided.
So let your heart begin to beat.

The Resurrection and the Life
Has at last visited your cave.
Take a breath,
Take a step of faith.
And rise up from this grave.

---

[29] John 11:43.

A Fingerprint of Love

Etched upon the earth's cold face
Is a fingerprint of love.
An undying mark of a dying Son
Of a Father up above.
A tree of bitter sacrifice
E'er rooted in this sod.
A cleansing blood
Of the ceaseless heart
Of the precious Lamb of God.

Throughout the pulsing ages,
His love broke through the night
And flooded this thirsting space of dust
With the glory of its light.
It conquered the whole of darkness
And took the keys of death.
It yet frees the seeking sinner
And snatches logic's breath.

It's acquainted with our grief
And can mend our wounded souls.
Its works uphold the power
Of the words writ in the scroll.
In the fires of our trials
It burns brighter still
And guides us to our purpose
With more passion and more zeal.

It calls to the heavy-ladened,
"Come lay your burdens down.
Come to the feet of Calvary,
Where redemption's song is found.

There pain will be eclipsed
And sorrows wiped away
In the glory of our Savior
On that eternal day."

His Grace Is Sufficient[30]

What is the price of our faith?
In his love and strength, we tarry.
We've been made alive but crucified
To the very cross we carry.

We've forsaken all to follow him,
To preach his love, in his name trust.
But why are nails in the hands that heal?
Why are thorns in the crowns of the just?

Why is our good answered with hate?
We are hated by all for his sake.[31]
Our faith is tried by striking means—
The prison, the furnace, the stake.

In weariness, in scorn, in hiding
We wander—
Our lives to our disgust.
Always in flesh, bearing Christ's death.
But his grace is sufficient for us.

For in our death, his life manifests.
In our weakness, we are made strong.
We can do all things,
All things through Christ.
Our eyes on the prize,
Our hope our song.

We are not alone, yes; and may

---

[30] Second Corinthians 12:9.
[31] Matthew 10:22.

That cloud of witness testify.
His grace may Paul continue praise.
His strength may Wurmbrand ever cry.

Always the need his grace did meet.
Always in fire, his power shown brighter.
We are more than conquerors through him.[32]
His will in triumph, the mightier.

So let us carry on bravely.
We're victorious in all, we trust.
There's temporal pain but eternal gain.
Yes, his grace is sufficient for us.

---

[32] Romans 8:37.

The Cry of Jeremiah

O Lord, you are stronger than I.
Your words come bursting out.
Your messages of warning
I cannot help but shout.

My old friends laugh with scorn.
They wait for me to slip.
They burn to quench the raging flame
Alive upon my lip.

I curse my day of birth.
My life is dark with shame.
My torment maddens me too long
To never speak your name.

My heart is weighed with grief.
My thoughts are wild and sore.
In the mires of my anguish,
I'll speak your words no more.

But you touched these lips of clay
And ignited in my soul
A consuming blaze of utterances
I just cannot control.

My heart begins to swell.
My spirit starts to groan.
I cannot quench this fire
Untamed within my bones.[33]

---

[33] Jeremiah 20:9.

My will must bow again.
Out comes your revelation.
Out comes your words of truth.
Out comes your desperation.

To save your scattered children
Within your precious sod,
Out comes the light of heaven.
Out comes the breath of God.

O Lord, you know our secrets.
You test the heart of man.
And like a mighty warrior,
Beside me you will stand.

My enemies can't triumph.
In captivity they'll sigh.
My God is my salvation,
So I'll praise his name on high.

We Too Will One Day Rise

How trials can overwhelm our souls!
How our thoughts strive to be sane
As we fight the fight and bear our blows!
How battles surge with endless flows
And exhaust our sighing brains!

How gusts rush with heavy tears of rain!
Where is our Lord above?
Does his sovereignty over all still reign?
How can we reconcile our pain
With the gracious God of love?

But our Father proved himself capable of
Reconciling all grievous woe
With the unfailing wonder of his love,
With a cross that reached heaven above
And pierced the earth below.

His heart poured out in redemption's flow
On the hill of Calvary.
When he gave his Son, his precious one!
Lo! His tear-stained face, his broken soul,
How acquainted with our grief!

But Christ rose again in victory.
So we, too, will one day rise.
How our souls will be forever free!
We'll sing for all eternity
With a heart that never dies!

I'm Taken at the Thought

What wrong have I committed
That this grief my right deserves?
The horrors of my anguish
Are a fire in my nerves.
Each story tears my spirit
With the vengeance of a scourge.
But my faith cannot be shaken
In the furies of this forge.

The bellows of the heavens
Roared against this frame of clay.
And the shadow of the lion
Set upon its guiltless prey.
Woe! The treasures of my being
Were devoured in a day.
But I'll praise the One who gave it
And took it now away.

It was you, most holy Sovereign
And ruler of all heaven,
Who introduced the challenge
To the accuser of our brethren.
You withdrew your mighty barrier
That enclosed my mortal space.
But to my knees I fell to worship,
And I blessed you to your face.

It was you who shaped the anvil
And caught me in your net.
And the furnace of affliction
For my testing you beset.
You swung your heavy hammer

And wrenched my center's threads.
It was you who caused the feet of men
To ride upon our heads.[34]

My very own betrayed me
And sold me as a slave.
But my journey to the Nile
Was the pathway you had paved.
You brought me through the fire.
You brought me through the flood.
The trials of my trekking
You're working for my good.

For now I know in part,[35]
But I'll continue to entreat.
My glass is dark as now,
But on that day I'll see complete.
And in the meantime, I will worship,
And at your feet, I'll bow.
You've done too many wonders
For me to doubt you now.

I know my Savior lives,
And on this sod, you'll stand at last.
In the splendor of your power
And a glory unsurpassed,
And face-to-face I'll see you,
And my pain will be as naught.
Yes, with my own eyes I'll behold you,
And I'm taken at the thought.

---

[34] Psalm 66:12.
[35] First Corinthians 13:9.

There's a Reason

There's a reason 'yond all reason,
Every moment, every day.
There's a hand discreetly guiding
Every step of every way.

There's an order of perfection
And a pattern 'yond all chance.
There's a meaning 'yond the question
Of the smallest circumstance.

There's a clock, divine in motion,
E'er defying random means.
There's a plan of perfect timing
And a God behind the scenes.

I Believe God

A storm descended on us
With a face set to assail.
The sea was overboiling
In the fury of the gale.
And darkened billows shrouded
The abode of heaven's light
For fourteens days of madness
And fourteen fearful nights.

The clouds were throwing tantrums
As their fists hurled hail around.
Like the mob that tried to stone me
At the gate of Zeus's town.
They dragged me out the city
As my life leaked through my stains.
But the fire of the Spirit
Was still racing through my veins.

God snatched me once again
From the clutches of grave's grip.
And an angel stood beside me
In that black hour on the ship.
His face beamed with the splendor
Of the light that changed my way.
His words were like the glory
Of the breaking of the day.

And I believe God.
He never failed me in this walk.
The ship may sink beneath me,
But I'm standing on the rock.
The serpent's bite can't harm me.

No weapon will succeed.
The battle is already won
The victory guaranteed.

So I'll sing his praise again,
Until my journey is complete,
And he shakes the prison grounds
Of my sore mortality.
My chains will drop behind me
And at last, I will be free.
And I'll dance in the reward
Of most blessed eternity.

Thy Gift of Peace

Thy peace, can human words describe?
I try yet to explain.
A ray of light within my soul
Through storms doth me sustain.

A calmness in the raging seas,
A hope when all seems lost.
A trust in him who guides my ways,
Assurance in the cross.

A rest, a stillness 'yond all fear,
A faith that conquers doubt.
I know not how, but I just know
Thou wilt work it all out.

Out of Them All

There are troubles that pull
At my heart like a weight.
I am lost in a sea
Of afflictions so great.
The waters are thick,
And the fire is hot.
But this blessed assurance
I haven't forgot.

That out of them all,
You deliver us, Lord,[36]
From the jaws of the lion,
From the edge of the sword.
From the spears of the jealous,
From the hands of the vile,
From prison and shipwreck,
Every heartache and trial.

You're with me in the fire;
I am never alone.
You call me to life,
And you roll back the stone.
I don't have to fear;
On your name I will call.
You deliver me, Lord,
From out of them all.

---

[36] Psalm 34:19.

I Am Persuaded

Come sweep me up
In your glory divine.
Let the life of your promise
Renew my mind.
In the thickness of fog,
Break through and shine.
Sustain me to the finish line.

The pressure proceeds,
But I press on with zeal.
My feet may tire,
But my faith is steel.
The fire fumes,
But I'll stand up and fight.
I'm secure in your love
And strong in your might.

I'll trust though you slay me,
My mind is made.[37]
I'm persuaded,
And I cannot be swayed.
No, nothing can part us
From your steadfast love,[38]
Not evils below nor angels above.

Not cares for today
Nor fears for tomorrow.
Not death nor danger

---

[37] Job 13:15.
[38] Romans 8:35.

Nor hunger nor sorrow.[39]
Strike the hammer and burn the old.
I'm coming out as pure as gold.

The flames are aggressive;
Your love is more fierce.
Your arms are wide open,
Your hands are pierced.
Your heart is as vast
As the span of the sea.
Your grace is the very
Air that I breathe.

Nothing can quench
The smile on your face.
I'm stirred again
To persist in my race.
Take heart, my soul,
You weary wanderer.
In Christ you're more
Than a conqueror.[40]

---

[39] Romans 8:35.
[40] Romans 8:37.

Like the Widow

Like the widow before the judge,
I present again my plea.
With iron determination
I wait on bended knee.

With new confidence I'm praying
With all my soul and might.
I'm zealous like the blind man,
Who cried out for his sight.

And I'm pressing like the woman
With the issue of blood,
As she fought her way against the rush
Of the surging of the flood.

I'm reaching out with desperate faith
To touch his garment's hem.
I will not rest until I get
My miracle from him.

And if I have to pour my box
I've bought with many years,
And lay all I am at his feet
And wipe them with my tears.

And if I have to disregard
The rules of pious men,
And forsake my pampered pride
And knock and knock again.

I'm determined for my breakthrough.
I refuse to stay the same.

Even a crumb will satisfy
This hunger in my flame.

So I'll march around my Jericho
And rip the roof apart.
His goodness will not disappoint
This longing in my heart.

He'll raise my dead soul from the grave
And set my spirit free.
Like the widow I'm persistent
As I pray on bended knee.

Try Again

Knock again, time again.
Get back up and try again.
The Spirit is alive within.
You were built to war and win.

Lift your eyes;
You weary rise.
Fix your gaze upon the prize.
Press on through the scars and sighs.
Get up after seven times.

Own success, pray victory.
Refuse to give in to defeat.
Some mountains were not meant to flee
But lay subdued beneath your feet.

The water stirs, so quickly run.
Your strength is in the holy one.
He will complete what he begun,
And the battle is already won.

Peniel

There you met me all alone
In the shadows of the camp.
And we wrestled till the moonlight
Ceased its throne to morning's lamp.
Each breath became a fire
That rekindled in my lung.
But my soul burned for that blessing
Alive upon your tongue.

My sweat poured down like rain.
But a fervor stirred within
That caused my heart to beat
Like I had drank adrenaline.
The blood rushed to my cheeks
As my want pursued to drive,
And I held onto your angel
As if clinging to my life.

We spent the hours struggling.
You put me to the test.
You tried the very bedrock
Of my hunger to be blessed.
You fought the very depths
Of my dogged desperation,
But you couldn't shake the clenches
Of my determination.

You wrenched my aching hip.
My desire just inflamed.
I knew you held the power
To change my problem's name.

And my reward dawned with the rising
Of the glory of the sun.
I wrestled face-to-face
With God and man and won.

He Has Overcome the World

Great the roar of these our giants.
Greater yet, the roar inside.
What are heights of earthen walls
When the Lord is on our side?

There is nothing that can harm us.
The destroyer's rage cannot contend.
The stronger man has won the battle,
And his name he will defend.

Great is the army that surrounds us,
But they are swallowed by the greater.
I'd fain endure these mortal's tests
Than the wrath of the Creator.

How hot the fire boiled!
But how his mighty works unfurled!
In this world we will have trouble,
But he has overcome the world.[41]

The weapons of our warfare
Will pull strongholds to their knees.
We will dance on heads of serpents
And divide the deepest seas.

And every knee shall bow before
His holy, matchless name.
Every mountain, every valley,
His great wonders we'll proclaim.

---

[41] John 16:33.

Until we reach the crowning mark
And praise through gates impearled,
In this world we will have trouble
But he has overcome the world.[42]

---

[42] John 16:33.

Be at Rest, Dear Worthy Traveler

Be at rest, dear worthy traveler.
Feel your weary soul restored.
Hear the choir of heaven singing.
Now inherit your reward.

Be free from pain and want and fear.
Be free from earthly strife.
Take of the great eternal fount,
Take of the tree of life.

Dance on streets of finest gold.
Be robed in purest white.
Be crowned and kissed with glowing rays
And streams of ceaseless light.

Enter gates of gleaming pearls.
Be filled with fervent fire.
Like the lamps before the ark, now shine
And sweep your singing lyre.

I'd fain exchange my earthly lot
To joy with you, my fair.
But here I'll run my temporal course
Until I meet you there.

Behold All Things Are New

In awe I am at the glorious thought
That forever 'fore his throne we'll make praise.
How fruitful our trials, the fights that we fought!
How worthwhile the trek for the prize of this gaze!
The abode of the Lord now with men doth dwell
What glory descends with all heavenly grace!
What majesty beyond all words to tell
Is the rapture that beams from his face!
And our tears shall forever be swept away
In the infinite ocean of his love.
Our sorrows and pain eclipsed on that day
In the triumph of the fire above.
In the embrace of the faithful and true,
The old is that, behold all things are new!